AF688210

Case Construction's Calculus

Building Winning Arguments and Structuring Effective Legal Presentations

Samantha Blackwell

Copyright © 2025 by Samantha Blackwell
All rights are reserved.

Contents

1 Chapter 1: Foundations of Argumentation

Logical reasoning forms the bedrock of any successful legal argument. It's not merely about presenting facts; it's about connecting those facts in a way that leads inexorably to your desired conclusion. Consider the classic syllogism: All men are mortal; Socrates is a man; therefore, Socrates is mortal. This simple structure illustrates the power of deductive reasoning, moving from general principles to specific conclusions. However, legal arguments rarely possess such stark simplicity. Inductive reasoning, moving from specific observations to broader generalizations, often plays a more significant role. For example, presenting numerous instances of similar behavior might lead you to argue a pattern of conduct. Understanding both deductive and inductive reasoning, and their limitations, is crucial for building a robust case. You must be aware of potential biases, both your own and those inherent in the evidence, ensuring a well-rounded analysis, devoid of logical fallacies. A common mistake is to commit an appeal to emotion, a fallacy where you persuade your audience based on feelings rather than reason. Always ground your arguments in solid logic, providing concrete evidence for every claim. A carefully constructed argument, built on a strong foundation of logic, is far more persuasive than one laden with emotional appeals.

Identifying the core issues is paramount. Before crafting a single sentence, thoroughly analyze the case. What are the legally relevant facts? What are the key legal questions the court must answer? Focusing on the central issues prevents your argument from becoming diffuse, losing its impact amidst a sea of irrelevant details. Clearly define the dispute, outlining the points of contention between the parties involved. Consider framing the central question as a specific, testable proposition. This makes it easier to gather evidence relevant to the question and construct a persuasive argument addressing it directly. The ability to distil complex factual scenarios into clear, concise statements of the core issues is a mark of skilled legal practitioners. This skill separates those who win cases from those who merely participate in them. It's not about piling up as much information as possible, but rather about efficiently and effectively presenting only what is strictly necessary and directly relevant to the core issues. Remember that clarity and focus win cases.

The process of defining these issues requires careful consideration. It's an iterative process; initial assumptions may be challenged or refined as more evidence is examined. Engage in thorough legal research, consulting statutes, case law, and other relevant materials to ensure a complete understanding of the applicable law. This research will reveal the legal standards against which the facts must be weighed and help refine your understanding of the crucial issues at stake. Consider the potential counterarguments, anticipating the other side's perspective to strengthen your own position. Preparing for these challenges makes your argument more resilient, able to withstand scrutiny. A comprehensive understanding of the relevant laws and precedents, combined with the ability to concisely articulate the core issues, is not just advantageous - it's essential for any aspiring lawyer. Ignoring this foundational step can lead to a disorganized, ineffective presentation that fails to resonate with the court.

Consider the burden of proof. Understand precisely what must be proven to succeed and which party carries that burden. This understanding directly informs the structure and content of your argument. If you're the plaintiff, you have the burden to demonstrate each element of your claim, providing sufficient evidence to meet the relevant standard of proof (preponderance of evidence, clear and convincing evidence, or beyond a reasonable doubt, depending on the nature of the case). Failure to address each element adequately weakens your entire case. This is especially true in cases involving multiple claims or multiple defendants. If you represent a defendant, your strategy might focus on refuting the plaintiff's evidence or demonstrating their failure to meet their burden of proof. Understanding the burdens of proof dictates the strategic direction of the entire case. It influences how you assemble your evidence, anticipate the other side's arguments, and structure your presentation to the court. Mastering this concept is essential to constructing a winning argument. Without a clear grasp of who has to prove what, your case risks becoming lost in a muddle of irrelevant facts.

1.1 Logical Reasoning

Deductive reasoning forms the bedrock of strong legal arguments. It involves starting with general principles (established laws, precedents) and moving towards a specific conclusion about the case at hand. Think of it as a logical pyramid, with established legal principles forming the broad base, and your case-specific conclusion resting neatly at the apex. A flawlessly constructed deductive argument is almost irrefutable, provided your premises are sound and your reasoning is impeccable. This requires meticulous attention to detail and a clear understanding of the relevant legal framework.

Inductive reasoning, conversely, builds from specific observations to broader generalizations. In legal contexts, this might involve presenting a series of facts–witnesses' testimonies, forensic evidence, documents–to establish a pattern or conclusion. However, unlike deductive reasoning, inductive reasoning doesn't guarantee absolute certainty; instead, it offers probabilities and strengthens your case through the accumulation of supportive evidence. The strength of your inductive argument hinges on the quality and quantity of evidence presented, its relevance to the case, and the absence of contradictory information. Careful selection and presentation are vital.

Understanding the difference is crucial. Deductive arguments provide irrefutable conclusions if the premises are true; inductive arguments, on the other hand, reach probable conclusions based on the weight of evidence. Successfully using both will allow you to build a formidable argument structure. For example, you might begin with deductive reasoning to establish the legal principles governing a particular area of law and then use inductive reasoning to show how the facts of your client's case fall squarely within

those principles, thereby achieving a compelling and robust legal argument.
Fallacies are errors in reasoning that undermine the validity of an argument. Recognizing and avoiding these errors is paramount to constructing sound legal arguments. Consider the fallacy of ad hominem, attacking the person making the argument rather than the argument itself. This tactic might feel tempting under pressure, but it's logically irrelevant and harms your credibility. Similarly, avoid the straw man fallacy, misrepresenting your opponent's position to make it easier to attack. Accurate and fair representation of opposing arguments demonstrates your intellectual honesty and strengthens your own case. Mastering the identification and avoidance of logical fallacies greatly enhances your persuasiveness and strengthens your position.
Beyond identifying fallacies, you must actively search for weaknesses in your own arguments. This seemingly counterintuitive step is invaluable. Identifying potential vulnerabilities allows you to preemptively address them, strengthening your position before your opponent even raises them. Anticipating counterarguments is key to presenting a comprehensive and robust case. This proactive approach transforms you from a reactive defender into a strategic planner, building a more solid and persuasive presentation. Critically analyzing your own case, looking for holes in logic and weak points in evidence, allows you to construct a far more resilient argument. This self-critique is not self-doubt, but rather a crucial part of strategic thinking and planning.
Consider the strength of your evidence. Is it direct or circumstantial? Direct evidence directly proves a fact (e.g., eyewitness testimony, a confession). Circumstantial evidence suggests a fact indirectly (e.g., footprints near a crime

scene). Understanding the distinctions is crucial to assessing the strength of your case and your opponent's. While both are admissible, direct evidence carries significantly more weight. However, a compelling collection of circumstantial evidence can prove immensely powerful, particularly if supported by expert testimony and carefully woven into a persuasive narrative. The key lies in strategically combining both types of evidence for the strongest impact.

The arrangement of your arguments also plays a crucial role. Beginning with your strongest points can immediately captivate your audience, setting a positive tone. Conversely, strategically placing weaker points– perhaps using them to transition to a more compelling argument – can mitigate their negative impact. It's about pacing, narrative flow, and building towards a crescendo, much like constructing a compelling story. Your arguments should form a cohesive, well-structured narrative, where each point supports and strengthens the overall argument. The goal isn't just to present facts; it's to tell a story that captivates and persuades.

In conclusion, logical reasoning is not simply about avoiding fallacies; it's about strategically constructing a comprehensive, persuasive argument using both deductive and inductive reasoning, proactively identifying weaknesses, strategically organizing your points, and carefully weighing the strength of your evidence. The mastery of these principles forms the foundation for building a winning case, ensuring your arguments are both sound and persuasive. By consciously applying these principles, you will enhance your ability to construct effective legal arguments, ensuring your position is not only legally sound but also strategically presented and undeniably impactful. Remember that building a winning argument is a multifaceted process requiring careful planning and execution.

1.2 Identifying Key Issues

Discerning the central issues within a case forms the bedrock of a successful legal strategy. It's not simply about identifying every detail; it's about pinpointing the truly critical elements that will determine the outcome. Failure to do so leads to disorganized arguments, wasted time, and ultimately, a weakened case. This precision requires a systematic approach, moving beyond surface-level understanding.

Start by meticulously reviewing all available evidence. This includes documents, witness statements, expert reports, and any other relevant materials. Don't just skim; actively engage with each piece, noting key facts, contradictions, and potential weaknesses. This painstaking process is essential, forming the raw material for your analysis. Remember, even seemingly insignificant details can sometimes unlock crucial insights. Treat every document and statement as potentially pivotal.

Next, carefully examine the legal framework applicable to the case. Identify the relevant statutes, case precedents, and legal doctrines. Understanding these will help you to frame the key issues within a clear legal context. This is where understanding the legal landscape is vital, it dictates the battlefield. Understanding the legal terrain allows you to anticipate potential challenges and strategically position your arguments. Legal research is crucial for this stage, ensuring a thorough comprehension of the applicable legal precedents and principles.

Once you've grasped the facts and the law, begin to synthesize the two. This involves identifying the points of contention – where the facts and the law clash or intersect. Ask yourself: What are the core disagreements between the parties? What specific legal elements must be proven to win the case? These questions will help you narrow your focus from a potentially wide range of issues to the most critical ones that will shape the outcome of the case. This is where your sharpest analytical skills are put to the test.

Now, prioritize the identified issues. Not all issues are created equal; some have a far greater impact on the overall outcome than others. Focus your efforts on the most significant ones – those that have the potential to either decisively win or lose the case. This prioritization requires sound judgment and an understanding of the broader legal strategy. A well-structured argument prioritizes efficiency, minimizing wasted resources on peripheral matters.

Finally, and critically, consistently revisit and refine your list of key issues. As the case progresses, new information may emerge, changing the strategic landscape. Remain flexible and adaptable, and be willing to adjust your focus as needed. Legal strategy is a dynamic process, demanding continuous evaluation and reassessment. This adaptive approach ensures your case remains focused and responsive to changes. The legal process is a marathon, not a sprint; consistent review is necessary. By following these steps and continuously refining your understanding of the key issues, you can construct a strong, focused, and persuasive argument that substantially increases your chances of success. This meticulous approach ensures that your efforts are concentrated on what truly matters, leading to a more effective and efficient use of time and resources. Remember, the core of effective advocacy lies in presenting a compelling case that focuses on the most impactful aspects of your client's situation.

2 Chapter 2: Structuring Your Case

A well-structured case is the backbone of any successful legal argument. It's not just about presenting facts; it's about arranging them to create a compelling and persuasive narrative. Choosing the right structure significantly impacts how your audience receives and interprets your argument. Consider your specific case details, legal issues, and the audience you're addressing.

The chronological approach, as its name suggests, presents the case in the order events unfolded. This method is particularly useful when the sequence of events is crucial to understanding the case's timeline and demonstrating causality. Imagine a personal injury case; a chronological structure would logically trace the accident from the initial incident, through medical treatment, to the present condition. This linear progression can build a powerful and easily understood narrative. However, this simplicity might not suit every case; if the details are complex or the key issues are dispersed across the timeline, other approaches might prove more effective.

Thematic organization offers a different approach. Instead of following a strict timeline, you group similar facts and arguments under specific themes.

This approach works well when your case has several key issues that need to be examined individually before weaving them together into a cohesive whole. For instance, in a contract dispute, you could organize your case around themes like breach of contract, damages, and mitigation. Each theme could then be fully explored before being integrated into your broader case strategy, offering a clear and focused argument. This approach ensures a sophisticated presentation of complex topics. Careful planning and a clear connection between the themes are crucial for avoiding a fragmented presentation.

The problem-solution method focuses on identifying the central problem and then presenting your solution. This framework is especially effective for cases that require a remedial action or a change in the status quo. For instance, in an environmental law case, you could begin by demonstrating the environmental damage caused by a particular action. Following this, you could detail how your proposed solution will mitigate the damage and prevent future occurrences. This approach requires a thorough understanding of the problem and a carefully developed and persuasive solution. In contrast to the chronological approach, this method may require rearranging the facts of your case to focus more on the proposed solution. The solution isn't merely a consequence of the problem; rather, it's the primary focus of your argument. Remember, the most effective structure isn't inherently one over the other; the optimal choice hinges on the unique characteristics of each case. You might even integrate elements from different approaches to craft a highly persuasive structure. For example, a case might benefit from a thematic organization of specific elements within a larger chronological framework, creating a structure tailored to its specific needs. Effective structuring requires a careful consideration of your case specifics, legal arguments, and desired impact on the audience. Choosing the right path isn't about memorizing methods; it's about applying strategic thinking and understanding your audience's needs. A successful legal argument is not simply a presentation of facts; it is a carefully crafted narrative. Therefore, understanding the strengths and weaknesses of different structural approaches allows you to present your arguments in the most persuasive way possible. This strategic choice contributes significantly to a winning case. The careful planning and thoughtful execution involved in structuring your case demonstrate a thorough understanding of your arguments and respect for the court's time and attention. Mastering these techniques enhances the clarity, coherence, and persuasiveness of your legal presentation. Remember that the selection of a structural approach is a crucial element in your preparation. Don't underestimate its significance.

2.1 Chronological Approach

A chronological approach structures your case by following the timeline of events. Imagine it as a story, unfolding naturally from beginning to end. This method is particularly effective when the sequence of events is crucial to understanding the case's core arguments. For instance, in a personal injury lawsuit, chronologically detailing the accident, subsequent medical treatment, and lasting effects creates a clear, compelling narrative. The judge or jury can easily follow the progression, understanding the cause and effect relationship between the defendant's actions and the plaintiff's injuries. This linear presentation can enhance comprehension and build a strong sense of credibility, avoiding any confusion or fragmented perception.

Consider a breach of contract case. Presenting the events in chronological order–from the signing of the contract, through the alleged breach, to the resulting damages–allows for a systematic presentation of evidence. Each stage builds upon the previous one, strengthening the overall argument and showcasing the clear trajectory of events leading to the plaintiff's claim. This method is particularly useful in establishing causation and damages, creating an undeniable link between the defendant's actions and the plaintiff's losses. However, a purely chronological approach isn't always ideal. If the case involves numerous, unrelated events, a strictly chronological presentation might feel disjointed and less impactful. In these situations, you might consider supplementing the chronological approach with thematic elements, grouping related events together to create a more focused narrative. For example, you could dedicate sections to specific issues, even if those issues happened at different points in time. This allows you to discuss related evidence together, reinforcing your arguments more effectively.

Remember, effective case construction often involves combining different approaches to suit the specific circumstances. While a chronological structure provides a clear roadmap for understanding the sequence of events, it's crucial to choose the method best suited to present the strongest, most persuasive narrative.

The beauty of the chronological approach lies in its inherent simplicity and understandability. It allows the audience to effortlessly follow the development of the case. This method is particularly useful in cases where proving the sequence of events is fundamental to proving liability or establishing damages. When used effectively, this structure naturally leads to a stronger conclusion, firmly grounding the final arguments in the established factual narrative. However, you must present the information clearly and concisely, ensuring the chronology serves to strengthen, not weaken your overall case. A well-structured chronological presentation ensures that your argument progresses logically, creating a natural flow that's easy to follow. This approach also helps prevent crucial pieces of information from being overlooked or presented out of context. The linear progression provides a framework for presenting your case, ensuring that each piece of evidence fits seamlessly into the narrative. Imagine trying to build a house without a blueprint; it's chaotic and inefficient. A chronological approach is your blueprint, guiding you and your audience toward a solid conclusion.

Moreover, this approach provides a clear structure to manage the complexity of a case. It can break down a multifaceted scenario into more easily digestible parts. Consider the complexity of a multi-party lawsuit. A chronological approach allows you to address the contributions and actions of each party in a logical and understandable sequence. This clarity helps the audience understand the interactions and relationships between the various actors involved. This simplifies a potentially confusing set of circumstances and enhances the overall clarity of your argument.

Finally, the chronological approach offers a powerful tool for building credibility. By sticking to the facts and presenting them in a logical order, you project an air of professionalism and competence. This strengthens your overall case and makes you appear more trustworthy and reliable in the eyes of the judge or jury. This method, when well-executed, can leave a lasting impression, solidifying your position as a credible and effective advocate.

2.2 Thematic Organization

Thematic organization offers a powerful alternative to chronological presentation. Instead of presenting facts in the order they occurred, you structure your argument around key themes or issues. This approach is particularly beneficial when dealing with complex cases involving multiple events or intertwined legal arguments; it allows for a more focused and persuasive presentation, preventing the audience from getting lost in a sea of dates and details. Think of it as building a case around central pillars, each supporting the overarching conclusion.

Imagine a negligence case involving a construction accident. A chronological approach would detail the sequence of events: the design phase, the construction process, the accident itself, and the aftermath. However, a thematic approach would group related facts under broader themes, such as inadequate safety measures, negligent supervision, or failure to comply with building codes. This allows you to build a stronger narrative around each specific issue, instead of simply presenting a timeline. For example, focusing on the inadequate safety measures, you could gather all evidence relevant to that theme, including expert testimony, photographs, and witness statements. This strategic grouping provides a clearer understanding of each distinct failure and their cumulative impact on the case.

This method facilitates a deeper understanding of each issue, allowing for more detailed examination. By isolating each theme, you can thoroughly explore its nuances and present compelling evidence supporting your argument. This deeper dive is vital for establishing causation and demonstrating the extent of the defendant's liability. Unlike a chronological presentation which might lose focus, a thematic approach enhances clarity and precision, thus making it easier for the judge or jury to follow the line of reasoning. Consequently, this method strengthens your overall argument considerably.

Consider using sub-themes within each major theme. Breaking down complex issues into smaller, manageable components allows for a more methodical and comprehensive examination. This layered approach helps maintain coherence and prevent the argument from becoming overly broad or diffuse. In our construction case, the "inadequate safety measures" theme could be further subdivided into specific areas such as insufficient scaffolding, lack of personal protective equipment (PPE), or failure to implement proper safety protocols. Each sub-theme would then be supported by relevant evidence, creating a well-structured and highly persuasive argument. This methodical approach enhances your case's persuasiveness significantly.

Furthermore, the thematic approach lends itself well to addressing anticipated counterarguments. You can directly counter opposing arguments within the relevant theme, streamlining the rebuttal and enhancing the overall flow of your presentation. Instead of interrupting your narrative with counterpoints at random points, you can present your rebuttals within the same thematic section, providing a more cohesive response. This allows you to effectively preemptively address potential challenges, showcasing preparedness and highlighting the strength of your arguments. This focused approach increases the overall persuasiveness of your presentation and significantly improves your credibility.

However, effective thematic organization requires careful planning and clear connections between the different themes. It is crucial to ensure a logical flow between the themes, avoiding abrupt transitions or disjointed arguments. A strong narrative should connect the various themes, demonstrating how they contribute to your overall conclusion. Moreover, avoid selecting themes that are unrelated or contradict each other, as this weakens the overall structure and detracts from the persuasiveness of your case. Creating a clear roadmap before you start outlining your arguments is essential.

The key is to choose themes that are relevant to the legal issues at hand and that allow for a clear and compelling narrative. Avoid themes that are too broad or too narrow. Select themes that will resonate with the audience and that you can support with solid evidence. This requires careful consideration of the facts of the case and the legal arguments involved. The selection process itself is integral to the success of your overall strategy. Carefully consider the central aspects of the case and structure your argument around them; remember that the overarching goal is to present a coherent and persuasive argument, and your choice of themes directly influences this goal.

Finally, consider your audience when selecting your themes. Present the information in a way that is easily understood and engaging for the judge or jury. Remember that even the strongest argument will fail if it's not presented clearly and effectively. Using plain language, clear visual aids and avoiding legal jargon, you'll strengthen your argument. By organizing your case thematically, you can create a presentation that is not only logically sound, but also easily understood and persuasive. This tailored approach to thematic organization will elevate the impact of your legal presentation substantially. This thoughtful consideration of your audience will increase the chances of your case being deemed successful.

2.3 Problem-Solution Method

The problem-solution method offers a straightforward, yet powerful, structure for presenting your legal case. It's particularly effective when the core of your argument centers on a demonstrable problem and your proposed solution directly addresses its root causes. Think of it as a narrative arc, moving from a clearly defined problem to a compelling solution, leaving the audience with a sense of resolution and understanding.

This method isn't just about outlining a problem and then presenting a solution. It requires a meticulous approach, carefully laying out the evidence that proves the existence and significance of the problem. You must meticulously detail the harm caused, presenting specific instances and data to paint a vivid picture of the problem's consequences. Don't rely on generalizations; use concrete examples to illustrate the extent of the damage. For instance, if you're arguing for increased safety regulations, don't simply state that the current regulations are insufficient. Instead, present specific accident reports, statistical data on injuries, and expert testimony to underscore the severity of the problem.

Next, you transition seamlessly into your proposed solution. This isn't simply a statement; it's a well-reasoned and thoroughly explained proposal. Your solution must directly address the previously established problem, offering a clear path towards mitigation or resolution. Highlight the feasibility and practicality of your solution, anticipating potential objections and proactively addressing them with persuasive counterarguments. Consider the resources required for implementation, the potential challenges, and how those challenges will be overcome. Perhaps a cost-benefit analysis can convincingly show the advantages of your approach.

Crucially, you need to demonstrate a direct causal link between your proposed solution and the mitigation of the identified problem. This is where strong logical reasoning comes into play, a concept you've already covered in earlier chapters. Avoid assumptions; clearly articulate the mechanism through which your solution will address the problem. If your solution involves a new law or policy change, for example, explicitly explain how this new legislation will directly address the identified flaws in the existing system, preventing future occurrences and mitigating existing harm.

Effective presentation is vital. Using visuals, such as charts and graphs, can powerfully illustrate the problem and the anticipated effects of your solution. A visual representation of accident statistics, for example, can have a far greater impact than a simple recitation of numbers. Remember the principles of effective visual aids discussed in Chapter 6.

Furthermore, consider the potential counterarguments your opponent might raise. Anticipate their objections and build them into your presentation, strategically addressing and refuting them before your opponent even has the chance. This proactive approach demonstrates your thoroughness and strengthens your overall argument. This is directly linked to the content of Chapter 5.

In essence, the problem-solution method is a persuasive tool that guides the audience through a logical progression, from the identification of a problem to the presentation of a viable solution, ultimately culminating in the conclusion that your proposed resolution is the most appropriate and effective course of action. Its effectiveness lies in its clear structure and the compelling narrative it creates, ensuring your argument is not only logically sound but also easily understood and persuasive. Remember to tailor this structure to your specific case, always ensuring the problem and solution are clearly defined and supported by compelling evidence. The clarity of your presentation, combined with the logical flow of your argument from problem to solution, will significantly enhance your chances of success.

3 Chapter 3: Crafting Compelling Narratives

Legal narratives aren't just about facts; they're about weaving a compelling story. Think of your case not as a dry recitation of evidence, but as a narrative with a beginning, a rising action, a climax, and a satisfying resolution. This requires more than just listing facts; it needs a clear trajectory that keeps the audience engaged and invested in the outcome. Your narrative should build momentum, drawing the listener into your client's experience, allowing them to connect emotionally and intellectually.

Unlike a simple chronological account, a compelling legal narrative selects and emphasizes details strategically. Don't overwhelm your audience with every single piece of information. Instead, focus on the key facts that support your argument, showcasing them in a way that creates a strong and clear picture. Think about how a skilled novelist carefully selects details to create atmosphere and suspense; do the same with your evidence. Remember, the goal isn't just to present the facts but to create a meaningful story around them. This ensures that the evidence doesn't just stand alone but becomes an integral part of a captivating narrative.

To truly connect with the judge or jury, your narrative must resonate emotionally. This doesn't mean manipulating emotions; it means presenting the human impact of the legal issue. Show, don't just tell, how the case affects real people's lives. A detailed account of your client's suffering, loss, or struggle, presented with empathy and sensitivity, can dramatically enhance the impact of your presentation. This isn't about being sentimental; it's about illustrating the real-world consequences, making the case relatable and memorable.

Credibility underpins everything. Maintain it diligently. Present your information accurately, supporting all claims with strong evidence. Avoid exaggeration or embellishment; rely instead on the power of clear, concise, and well-supported arguments. Acknowledge weaknesses in your case honestly and address them head-on, showing your audience that you're confident and forthright. By handling any potential challenges openly, you can significantly bolster your credibility. A credible narrator is more convincing, even when dealing with difficult subject matters.

Engaging your audience means understanding their perspectives and tailoring your story accordingly. Think about who you're addressing: a seasoned judge, a jury of everyday citizens, or an arbitration panel. Adjust your language, tone, and level of detail to suit their understanding and expectations. Use vivid language and compelling imagery to keep them focused and invested in your narrative. Remember to maintain consistent eye contact and incorporate variations in your tone of voice to create engagement. In essence, building a strong connection with your audience helps cement your presentation's lasting impact.

Remember, the power of storytelling lies in its ability to simplify complexity, to make the abstract tangible, and the intangible understandable. By harnessing the art of storytelling, you transform a dry recitation of facts into a persuasive, engaging, and ultimately winning argument. Your legal case is not just a series of events; it's a story with a beginning, a middle, and a crucial end. This final point underscores the importance of not only presenting your case but doing so in a manner that is both effective and unforgettable. By crafting a narrative that is compelling, emotional, and credible, you significantly enhance your chances of a positive outcome.

3.1 Storytelling Techniques

Human beings are naturally drawn to stories. We understand the world through narratives, absorbing information and forming connections more readily when presented in a compelling story format. This inherent predisposition makes storytelling an incredibly powerful tool for legal professionals. A well-crafted narrative not only presents the facts but also engages the emotions, creating a lasting impact on the judge or jury. Think of it this way – a dry recitation of facts is far less likely to resonate than a narrative that paints a picture, evokes empathy, and leaves a lasting impression.

The key is to construct a narrative arc that mirrors the structure of a classic story. Begin with an engaging introduction that immediately captures attention; think of it as setting the stage for your case. Perhaps you start with a vivid description of the scene, introducing the central characters and the conflict at hand. This initial hook needs to be strong enough to grab the audience and keep them invested in the subsequent development of your case. Don't underestimate the power of grabbing their attention from the very beginning; it's crucial for setting the tone and building anticipation.

Next, build the tension. This is where you carefully present your evidence, weaving a narrative that gradually reveals the complexities of the situation. Each piece of evidence contributes to the overall picture, building momentum as you move towards the climax of your story. Don't just present facts; show how these facts fit into the larger narrative, highlighting connections and implications. Consider using metaphors and analogies to create engaging illustrations and make complex information easier to comprehend.

The climax is the point of highest tension. It's the moment where the crucial pieces of evidence come together, demonstrating the strength of your case and refuting the opposing arguments. This is not simply about presenting the evidence; it's about orchestrating a powerful reveal that leaves the audience with a clear and unshakeable understanding of your argument's validity. This carefully planned sequence of events, this building of suspense, enhances the impact and memorability of your evidence.

Then comes the resolution. Here, you bring everything together, summarizing your key points and restating the conclusions of your narrative. The resolution isn't merely a rehashing of facts; it's a synthesis of everything you've presented, demonstrating the logical and emotional coherence of your story. This is your opportunity to leave a lasting impression, reinforcing the strength of your case and solidifying the argument in the minds of the judges or jury members. A well-crafted resolution leaves the audience feeling satisfied, convinced, and persuaded. It's the final note of your carefully composed symphony of facts and narrative.

Finally, remember your audience. Tailor your storytelling to resonate with their values and experiences. Understanding your audience's perspective allows you to shape your narrative in a way that is both persuasive and emotionally resonant. What will connect with them most effectively? What kind of story will they find compelling and memorable? The more you understand your audience, the more effectively you can use storytelling to sway their judgments. Empathy and understanding are not just emotional qualities; they are crucial tools in persuasive storytelling.

Consider using different narrative voices and perspectives. You might use a first-person narrative to create a more intimate connection with your audience, immersing them in the experiences of those involved in the case. On the other hand, a third-person narrative might provide a sense of objectivity, allowing you to present facts and evidence in a detached and neutral manner. The choice of narrative voice should depend on the specifics of your case and the desired emotional impact. Experiment with these approaches and observe how they affect the reception of your presentations.

Another powerful technique is foreshadowing. By subtly hinting at future events or developments, you can build suspense and anticipation, making your narrative more engaging and memorable. This element of anticipation is a crucial element in constructing a persuasive narrative that keeps the audience hooked throughout your presentation. Think of it like leaving intriguing clues that gradually reveal themselves throughout your presentation, leaving them constantly engaged and eager to learn more.

Remember that storytelling is not about embellishing or manipulating facts. It's about presenting the truth in a compelling and engaging way. Authenticity is critical; a fabricated story will not resonate with the audience and can significantly damage your credibility. The power of a narrative lies in how it illuminates and frames the truth, transforming mere facts into a compelling and unforgettable story. Honesty is, therefore, as crucial as your ability to frame a narrative effectively. It is the bedrock upon which your credibility is built.

Your storytelling should always serve to clarify and amplify the evidence, not to obscure it. Use narrative techniques to illuminate the facts, making them easier to understand and more emotionally resonant. Do not let the story overshadow the evidence; instead, use it as a tool to present the evidence in a more powerful and persuasive way. Remember: the aim is to construct a narrative that supports and strengthens your legal argument, not to distract from it. This should always be your guiding principle.

3.2 Emphasizing Key Evidence

Highlighting crucial evidence isn't merely about presenting facts; it's about weaving them into a compelling narrative that resonates with your audience. Consider the impact of a single, powerfully presented piece of evidence versus a barrage of loosely connected details. The former is far more memorable and persuasive. Think of it like a skilled storyteller–they don't just recount events; they carefully select details to build suspense, reveal character, and ultimately, move their audience. You, as the legal advocate, must do the same.

Effective emphasis hinges on context. Don't simply present evidence; frame it within the broader narrative of your case. Show how each piece fits into the larger picture, building a solid, irrefutable foundation for your argument. For instance, if you're arguing negligence, don't just present the evidence of the accident; show how the defendant's actions or inactions directly caused it, highlighting the causal link with precision. This contextualization is key to making your evidence truly impactful.

Beyond simple presentation, consider the order in which you introduce evidence. Start with your strongest pieces–the ones that instantly grab attention and establish the core of your argument. Then, strategically build upon this foundation, using subsequent evidence to reinforce your claims and address potential counterarguments proactively. Think of it as a pyramid; you begin with a strong base and build upwards, creating a structure that's both impressive and unwavering. A chaotic presentation, on the other hand, risks losing the jury or judge in a sea of information.

Visual aids play a crucial role. A well-crafted chart or a clear photograph can dramatically enhance the impact of your evidence, transforming complex data into easily digestible information. Remember, however, that visuals should complement, not replace, your verbal presentation. They are there to enhance understanding, not to do the heavy lifting. Avoid overwhelming your audience with too much visual information; instead, focus on presenting only the most relevant and persuasive data. Think of it as showcasing the most impactful jewels, not an entire chest.

Don't underestimate the power of repetition, but use it judiciously. Reiterating key pieces of evidence throughout your presentation can embed them in your audience's memory, strengthening your overall argument. However, avoid monotonous repetition; instead, weave the key evidence into different parts of your narrative, each time highlighting a different facet or connection. This approach avoids dullness and enhances impact, leaving your audience more likely to remember and believe.

Your delivery is equally vital. Speak with conviction, but also with clarity and honesty. Your tone, body language, and emphasis all influence how your audience receives the evidence. If you present evidence hesitantly or with uncertainty, it will undermine its power, making your case appear weaker. Project confidence, even if you're internally nervous. This confidence is contagious and can subtly shift your audience's perception of the validity of your points.

Finally, anticipate and address potential objections. By preemptively acknowledging weaknesses in your evidence and offering counterarguments, you demonstrate foresight and strengthen your credibility. This approach, while appearing risky, can disarm opponents and subtly guide the narrative in your favor. This strategic approach showcases your preparedness and bolsters your overall case. Remember, handling possible counterarguments isn't about admitting defeat; it's about demonstrating thoroughness and control. Addressing these head-on demonstrates strength and confidence.

3.3 Emotional Resonance

Emotional resonance isn't about manipulating emotions; it's about connecting with the human experience at the heart of every legal case. A compelling narrative doesn't just present facts; it reveals the impact those facts have on real lives, making the abstract legal concepts relatable and meaningful to the judge or jury. Think of it like this: you're not just presenting a case, you're sharing a story.

Consider the plaintiff in a personal injury case. Their injuries aren't just medical terms and statistics; they're limitations on daily life, lost opportunities, and emotional distress. By focusing on the lived reality of the plaintiff's experience, their struggle becomes palpable, their pain relatable. This is where you weave in the emotional element. Describe the daily struggles, the missed milestones, the emotional toll the injury has taken. Use vivid descriptions, not just cold, clinical details. Paint a picture with your words. Avoid hyperbole; authenticity is key.

Empathy is crucial. It's not about feeling what your client feels, but understanding their feelings. Understanding their pain, their frustration, their fear, and their hope. By understanding these emotions, you can articulate them in a way that resonates with the audience. This isn't manipulation; it's human connection. It's about demonstrating that you understand the human cost of the legal dispute, not merely the legal complexities. This connection fosters trust and belief in your case.

Remember, even in seemingly dry corporate litigation, there's often a human element. Perhaps a small business is facing bankruptcy, a family's livelihood is at stake, or a community is threatened by environmental damage. Uncovering and showcasing this human element will dramatically increase the impact of your case, making it far more persuasive than a purely logical presentation. It adds weight, depth, and undeniable power.

However, this doesn't mean abandoning logic or facts. Emotional resonance should complement, not replace, the solid legal foundation of your argument. The emotional element strengthens the core message by making it unforgettable and impactful. It's the difference between a case that is understood and a case that is felt. Think of it as seasoning a dish–a pinch of emotional resonance makes the factual basis of your case significantly more palatable and persuasive to your audience.

Furthermore, remember your audience. Judges and juries are not simply passive recipients of information; they are people with their own experiences and emotions. They want to see the human impact of the case. They want to understand not just the "what," but also the "why" and the "how" – the implications on the individual involved and the wider community. By strategically appealing to their shared human experience, you create a strong connection that transcends the legal technicalities. The more genuine the connection, the more powerful the argument.

The goal isn't to pull at heartstrings with manipulative tactics; it's to present a truthful and relatable narrative that embodies the emotional reality of the situation. Therefore, always ground your emotional appeals in the evidence you have presented. Never let emotional appeals overshadow the legal framework supporting your case. Consider the potential counterarguments and address them directly. A well-structured and logically sound case strengthened by emotional resonance is far more likely to achieve success than one that relies solely on either.

Finally, practice and preparation are paramount. Rehearsing your presentation allows you to refine your delivery and ensure the emotional elements are seamlessly integrated into the overall argument. Practice helps you deliver your narrative with conviction and sincerity. Authenticity is paramount; an insincere attempt at emotional resonance will backfire. So, work on your delivery, craft your narrative carefully, and let the human element shine through. The results will speak for themselves. Your ability to connect with the jury or judge on a human level will elevate your presentation significantly, making your case resonate long after the closing arguments. The blend of reasoned logic and genuine emotional connection is the key to building a truly winning case.

3.4 Maintaining Credibility

Maintaining credibility is paramount; it's the bedrock upon which your entire case rests. Without it, even the most meticulously structured argument, the most compelling narrative, and the most powerfully presented evidence will crumble. Think of it as the invisible glue holding your case together, ensuring that every piece fits perfectly and conveys a message of trustworthiness. Your credibility isn't solely dependent on the factual accuracy of your claims, although that is certainly a vital component. It also hinges on your demeanor, your presentation style, and even the subtle choices you make in structuring your arguments. Projecting an air of confidence, not arrogance, is key. Hesitation or uncertainty can undermine your authority. Preparation is essential. Thorough research not only strengthens your arguments but demonstrates your diligence and commitment to the case, thus reinforcing your credibility.

The way you present yourself physically also plays a crucial role. Maintain professional attire and posture. Avoid distracting mannerisms like fidgeting or excessive hand gestures; these can subtly communicate a lack of confidence and diminish your authority. Conversely, confident posture and purposeful gestures can enhance your presence and make you appear more convincing. Maintaining consistent eye contact, appropriate for the cultural context of the courtroom, connects you with the jury or judge, fostering a sense of trust and engagement.

Honesty and transparency are equally vital. While you're naturally advocating for your client, outright deception will irrevocably damage your reputation. Avoid exaggerating facts or misrepresenting evidence. Instead, present your arguments in a straightforward and transparent manner. If you're unsure about a particular point, acknowledge it openly rather than trying to gloss over it. Such honesty showcases integrity, which builds trust and reinforces your credibility.

Addressing opposing arguments head-on demonstrates your preparedness and strengthens your credibility. Don't shy away from acknowledging valid counterpoints, but always do so strategically. Rather than dismissing them outright, acknowledge the opposing argument's merit before refuting it with your own evidence and reasoning. This approach demonstrates intellectual honesty and fairness, crucial elements for building trust with the jury or judge.

Moreover, consider your language carefully. Avoid overly technical jargon, particularly if you are addressing a lay audience. Aim for clarity and precision, selecting language your audience can easily understand. Avoid inflammatory language; maintain a professional and respectful tone even when dealing with contentious issues. Using accessible language makes you more relatable and establishes a bond with your audience, indirectly bolstering your credibility.

Even seemingly small details impact your perceived credibility. The precision of your citations, the thoroughness of your documentation, the organization of your materials–these all subtly influence your audience's perception of your competence and trustworthiness. Sloppiness in these areas suggests a lack of care and thoroughness. This can inadvertently undermine your credibility even before you begin presenting your arguments.

In conclusion, maintaining credibility is a holistic process. It's not simply about stating facts correctly; it's about cultivating a presence that inspires trust and confidence. It's about presenting yourself as a competent, prepared, honest, and respectful advocate. This is achieved through careful preparation, thoughtful presentation, and genuine integrity. Remember, your credibility isn't just a component of your case; it's the foundation upon which its success rests. Nurture it, protect it, and let it work for you in every aspect of your legal presentation. Your actions, your words, and your demeanor–all contribute to building and sustaining that crucial element of trust that underpins every winning argument. Cultivate a reputation for honesty and fairness, and let that reputation work for you.

3.5 Audience Engagement

Your audience isn't just a passive recipient of information; they are active participants in the construction of your argument. Engaging them effectively is not merely about presenting facts; it's about creating a connection, fostering understanding, and building trust. Consider this chapter as your guide to transforming passive listeners into active allies in your case.

Direct engagement often begins long before you step into the courtroom. Thorough research into your audience–their background, biases, and potential areas of skepticism—is crucial. Understanding their perspectives allows you to tailor your approach, anticipating their questions and addressing their concerns proactively. You're building a bridge, not erecting a wall. A well-researched presentation shows respect for your audience's intellect and time. The language you use plays a crucial role. Avoid legal jargon whenever possible; opt for clear, concise, and accessible language that everyone can understand. This doesn't mean oversimplifying your argument; it's about making it understandable without sacrificing intellectual rigor. Employing analogies and relatable examples can help make complex legal concepts more easily digestible, turning abstract ideas into tangible realities within their grasp.

Storytelling transcends the mere recitation of facts. A compelling narrative imbues your argument with emotional weight, making it memorable and persuasive. By weaving together evidence and narrative, you create a coherent and engaging experience. This helps to create emotional resonance, making your case not just intellectually sound but also deeply human, fostering empathy and connecting with the audience on a personal level.

Maintaining eye contact is more than just a matter of politeness; it's a powerful tool for connection. By making eye contact with individual members of the audience, you create a sense of personal connection, drawing them into your presentation and ensuring their attention. Varying your tone and pace is equally important; a monotonous delivery can quickly lose an audience's attention. Remember, you're not just presenting information; you're having a conversation.

Incorporate visual aids judiciously. While charts and graphs can be helpful, avoid overwhelming your audience with excessive detail. Keep visuals clear, concise, and relevant to your argument. The goal is to enhance your presentation, not to distract from it. Overly complex visuals can become a distraction, turning your audience's focus away from your core message.

Actively encourage audience participation. Asking open-ended questions, pausing for responses, and acknowledging feedback demonstrate respect for their input and engagement. A skilled lawyer uses these interactions to further strengthen their position. This isn't just about acknowledging their presence; it's about making them active participants. This process often clarifies aspects of the case that might not have been immediately apparent, enriching the discourse and improving understanding.

Mastering the art of audience engagement is an ongoing process. It requires practice, self-reflection, and a genuine commitment to connecting with your audience on a human level. Remember, persuasive legal arguments are not won solely through impeccable logic and flawless legal reasoning; they're also won through the ability to connect with those who hold the power to decide your case's fate. The best legal presentations are not simply heard, but are experienced, remembered, and acted upon. That experience begins with your ability to capture and maintain their attention. In essence, audience engagement is the cornerstone of effective legal persuasion. This, combined with clear and logical argumentation, offers a path to successful legal advocacy.

4 Chapter 4: Presenting Evidence Effectively

Effective presentation of evidence is paramount to a successful legal case. It's not enough to simply possess strong evidence; you must present it in a way that resonates with the judge or jury, convincing them of its relevance and credibility. This requires careful planning and execution, understanding the nuances of both document presentation and witness examination.

Document presentation isn't just about handing over papers; it's about storytelling through documents. Organize your documents logically, perhaps chronologically to show a clear timeline of events, or thematically to highlight specific arguments. Use clear and concise summaries to precede the actual documents, highlighting the key information and its relevance to your case. This is crucial to help navigate the potentially overwhelming amount of information that may be involved, making sure your core points are easily highlighted. Remember that concise summaries, clearly presented, are extremely effective. Make it simple to understand for the audience. Avoid overly technical jargon; translate complex information into plain language, ensuring everyone can comprehend it and therefore be convinced by your argument.

Consider the use of visual aids. Charts, graphs, and timelines can transform complex information into easily digestible visuals, making your points more memorable and impactful. A simple chart showing a trend, for example, can be far more persuasive than a page of dense data. However, keep the visuals simple and uncluttered; they should enhance your argument, not detract from it. Always remember to explain the information within the visual, don't just present them alone. Never assume your audience will fully comprehend them automatically.

Moving to witness examination, effective questioning is a skill honed through practice and preparation. Before the examination, thoroughly review the witness's statement and identify potential weaknesses or inconsistencies. Your goal isn't merely to elicit facts; it's to present a coherent narrative that supports your case. You need to guide the witness through a carefully constructed path, leading them to the conclusions that support your argument. Remember to keep your questions clear, concise, and focused. Avoid leading questions, which can undermine your credibility, instead phrasing your questions in open-ended style, allowing the witness to answer in their own words. This will maintain a more neutral tone and allow the witness's honest response to help support your argument.

Anticipate opposing counsel's line of questioning and prepare your witness to address those challenges confidently and truthfully. Rehearsing answers is crucial; while this should not be aiming to create a robotic recital, it helps ensure the witness remains consistent in their testimony and avoid contradictions or uncertainties which can significantly weaken the case. Focus your questions on specific, relevant aspects of the witness testimony. This prevents rambling and keeps the examination focused on the vital elements of your case, ensuring the witness's contribution is fully used to support your argument. The aim is not just to elicit information, but to construct a compelling narrative and present a convincing case.

During the examination, maintain a professional demeanor, even when facing challenging or unexpected responses. Control the pace of the examination, allowing ample time for answers but keeping the proceedings focused and efficient. Remember that your aim is to present the information as effectively as possible, and that maintaining a polite and professional attitude assists with this, preventing any unnecessary arguments or disruptions. This keeps the focus on the evidence itself, without needless confrontations and interruptions.

Effective evidence presentation is not a standalone skill; it's intertwined with other aspects of legal advocacy. The narrative crafted in Chapter 3 should directly inform your evidence selection and presentation. The structural framework discussed in Chapter 2 should guide the order of your evidence. Addressing opposing arguments, as discussed in Chapter 5, will often require strategic use of evidence to refute counterclaims. Ultimately, remember that presenting evidence is about persuasion; it's about weaving together facts, documents, and witness testimony to create a compelling and convincing case.

The strategic use of evidence is a powerful tool in legal advocacy. Mastering these techniques requires both preparation and skillful execution. By approaching evidence presentation systematically and thoughtfully, you can significantly enhance the persuasiveness of your case and increase your chances of success. Remember, successful legal advocacy is a blend of many crucial elements. This chapter, in conjunction with the others in the book, provides a comprehensive guide to constructing a winning argument and delivering a persuasive legal presentation.

4.1 Document Presentation

Selecting the right documents is paramount. Don't overwhelm the court with irrelevant paperwork. Instead, meticulously choose only those documents directly supporting your argument, prioritizing clarity and conciseness above all else. Think of it like sculpting; you're chipping away at unnecessary details to reveal the core strength of your case. Each document should be a hammer blow, striking precisely at the heart of your opponent's weakness.

Preparation is key. Before presenting any document, thoroughly review it yourself. Understand every sentence, every detail. Identify potential points of counter-argument. Anticipate questions your adversary might raise. This preemptive preparation will allow you to confidently and competently address any challenges during the presentation. You'll be ready to smoothly deflect any attempts to undermine your evidence.

Organization is crucial for a seamless presentation. Chronological order often works best, presenting documents in the sequence of events. This creates a narrative flow, making it easy for the judge or jury to follow. Alternatively, a thematic approach can be effective, grouping documents based on similar evidence or legal issues. Choose the method that best supports the storyline of your case, emphasizing coherence and a compelling narrative. Remember, the goal is to make the story clear and easy to understand.

Highlighting key information within the documents is critical. Use annotations, markers, or even prepared summaries to emphasize the most relevant points. Don't simply present the document; guide the audience to the specific passages that solidify your arguments. This focus helps avoid unnecessary distractions and ensures the critical information is not lost amidst the volume of other documents and text. Your annotations become a silent storyteller, guiding the audience to your most powerful points.

Presenting the documents themselves requires strategy. Avoid simply reading the document aloud. Instead, summarize and contextualize each document before introducing it, framing it within your broader argument. Use visual aids if appropriate, such as a projector or large-screen monitor, to ensure everyone in the court can easily view the evidence. This adds clarity and professionalism to your presentation and makes it much more digestible for the audience.

Handling objections gracefully is essential. Expect your adversary to raise objections. Prepare for these challenges by understanding the rules of evidence. If an objection is valid, concede gracefully; you'll maintain credibility. If you believe the objection is invalid, respond calmly and confidently, explaining why the document is admissible. Your poise under pressure will show your mastery of the process and leave a positive impression on the court.

Consider your audience. Remember that legal professionals and judges often possess a high degree of knowledge; don't patronize them. However, also remember that even experienced professionals need clarity and succinctness in your presentation. Tailor your explanations to ensure comprehension while remaining precise and efficient. Never compromise on clarity for the sake of brevity.

Finally, practice, practice, practice. Rehearse your presentation multiple times, including the introduction, summary, and responses to potential objections. This preparation will enhance your comfort and confidence, leading to a smoother, more persuasive presentation. A well-rehearsed presentation conveys expertise and builds credibility in the courtroom or any legal setting. Remember: effective document presentation is not just about the documents themselves; it's about telling a compelling story through them.

4.2 Witness Examination

Effective witness examination is the cornerstone of a successful case. It's not merely about asking questions; it's about orchestrating a narrative, painting a picture for the judge or jury using the witness's testimony. This involves careful planning, strategic questioning, and an acute awareness of the nuances of human communication. Remember, your goal isn't just to elicit information; it's to present that information in a compelling and persuasive manner.

Before you even step into the courtroom, meticulous preparation is key. Thoroughly review your witness's statement, identifying both strengths and potential weaknesses. Anticipate the opposing counsel's line of questioning, formulating strategies to address potential challenges proactively. Consider different approaches to elicit the necessary information, remembering that different individuals respond differently to various questioning styles. Some witnesses might respond better to open-ended questions, while others thrive under more structured questioning. Practice your examination with the witness beforehand to build rapport and ensure a smooth flow during the actual testimony. This preparation will allow you to react quickly and confidently to unexpected developments.

During the examination, maintain control. Begin with simple, straightforward questions, building trust and establishing a baseline of credibility. Your tone should be calm, professional and respectful, but assertive. This is essential to projecting confidence and credibility. Avoid leading questions which may taint the testimony and could be inadmissible. Your questions should guide the narrative without dictating the answers. This will help you steer the witness towards your desired outcome without seeming to manipulate the truth. Listen intently to every answer; the unexpected can provide valuable clues or open up new avenues for questioning, allowing for a more flexible and effective approach.

Addressing potential challenges is critical. If the witness falters or makes a mistake, address it calmly and strategically, without appearing to attack them. A gentle redirection or a rephrasing of the question may be sufficient to bring them back on track. Remember, the objective is to present a cohesive and convincing narrative, not to publicly humiliate the witness. Think of this as a delicate dance, requiring tact and sensitivity. It is better to recover from an unforeseen issue and to calmly correct any inconsistencies than to lose your control and to become aggressively confrontational.

Remember the importance of visual aids. Sometimes, a simple diagram or a photograph can clarify a point or bring the testimony to life. But use such visuals sparingly, focusing only on those that enhance the witness's testimony. Overusing them can detract from the impact of the testimony itself. These aids should never be used to overwhelm the witness or confuse the jury. Keep it concise and relevant to prevent confusion.

Your closing questions should be designed to reinforce the key points of the witness's testimony, leaving a lasting impression on the judge or jury. Summarize the important aspects of their testimony, reiterating those points that directly support your case. You should never ask a witness something that you cannot answer yourself. This approach provides a solid and unwavering foundation for your argument.

Finally, it is crucial to always maintain ethical conduct. Never mislead the witness, coach them improperly, or present information that you know is false. Your integrity is paramount. Your reputation and the integrity of your profession are at stake. A successful witness examination depends on your preparation, your skill, your tact, and most importantly, your adherence to ethical guidelines. Remember, honesty and preparation are the cornerstones of a compelling and successful legal strategy. This careful attention to detail, this thoughtful preparation, and this careful execution will be reflected in the quality of your work and in the success of your cases. The impact of effective witness examination goes far beyond just a single case; it reflects a dedication to the pursuit of justice and the ethical practice of law.

5 Chapter 5: Addressing Opposing Arguments

Confronting opposing arguments isn't about dodging the issue; it's about strategically integrating them into your own narrative. Ignoring counterarguments leaves gaping holes in your case, inviting your opponent to exploit vulnerabilities. Instead, anticipate potential criticisms. Imagine yourself in your adversary's shoes–what are their strongest points? What evidence might they present? Thoroughly researching the opposing side's potential arguments is crucial; it's the difference between a reactive defense and a proactive, well-structured presentation.

A strong defense begins with recognizing the validity of some opposing points. Strategic concession acknowledges the opponent's arguments without surrendering your position. For example, if the opposing counsel presents a seemingly compelling piece of evidence, acknowledging its relevance, while simultaneously contextualizing it within the larger picture, demonstrates fairness and strengthens your credibility. It allows you to disarm your opponent by showing you've considered their perspective, making your subsequent refutation more convincing.

Refuting counterarguments requires more than simply stating the opposing claim is wrong. To effectively dismantle an opposing argument, you must address it directly, using sound logic and compelling evidence. Employing logical fallacies to counter the other side's arguments undermines your own case. Instead, focus on providing a clear and concise explanation of why the opposing claim is flawed, perhaps citing case law, expert testimony, or verifiable data to support your refutation. Remember, brevity and clarity are key in legal arguments. A convoluted refutation only confuses the audience and weakens your case.

Consider the impact of your language. Avoid inflammatory language; maintain a professional tone, even when dealing with contentious points. Remember that your delivery is just as crucial as the content itself. A calm, measured approach enhances your credibility, even if the topic is emotionally charged. Moreover, demonstrating respect towards the opposing counsel doesn't weaken your position; instead, it enhances your professional demeanor and strengthens your case's overall persuasiveness.

Let's say the opposing counsel argues that a crucial witness is unreliable due to prior convictions. Instead of dismissing their concerns outright, you could acknowledge the witness's past mistakes, but then highlight their recent rehabilitation, perhaps citing their consistent testimony, or corroborating evidence to bolster their credibility. This approach acknowledges the potential weakness while minimizing its impact. By demonstrating a nuanced understanding of the evidence, you not only neutralize the opposition's argument but also solidify your case.

Always keep the audience in mind. Remember that your goal is not just to refute the opposing argument but also to persuade the judge or jury. Tailor your response to their perspective and understanding. Avoid complex legal jargon if the audience is unfamiliar with such terminology. Using plain language, supported by clear examples and logical reasoning, ensures that your message is easily understood and resonates with the intended audience. A successful refutation demonstrates your understanding of the subject matter and your ability to address complex issues in a clear, concise, and persuasive manner.

Furthermore, preparation is paramount. Spend sufficient time anticipating potential counterarguments and developing effective responses. This proactive approach ensures that you're not caught off guard, allowing for a more confident and well-articulated response. Practicing your presentation, including the anticipated rebuttals, greatly enhances your delivery and confidence in court. Don't let the opposing arguments dictate the flow of your case; instead, incorporate them strategically into your overarching narrative, showcasing your preparedness and command of the situation. The ability to expertly handle opposing arguments transforms a reactive defense into a proactive, persuasive approach that significantly enhances your chances of success. Remember, skillful handling of opposing arguments isn't just about winning; it's about building a solid, irrefutable case.

5.1 Anticipating Rebuttals

Effective case construction isn't just about presenting your own arguments; it's about anticipating and skillfully dismantling the opposition's. Ignoring potential counterarguments leaves your case vulnerable, resembling a poorly fortified castle waiting to be breached. Your preparation must extend beyond crafting a compelling narrative; it must encompass a preemptive strike against the opposing counsel's likely lines of attack.

Consider the opposing counsel's perspective. What evidence might they use? What weaknesses might they exploit in your case? You might find it helpful to role-play, taking on the role of your opponent and building their case against yours. This exercise will unveil blind spots in your own strategy. A truly effective advocate doesn't just build their case; they deconstruct the opponent's, anticipating every move and strategically neutralizing their impact. This proactive approach will bolster your confidence and allow you to maintain control of the narrative.

Remember, anticipating rebuttals isn't about inventing arguments out of thin air; it's about a thorough analysis of your own case's vulnerabilities. Ask yourself: what are the weakest points of my evidence? Are there any logical gaps in my reasoning that the other side could exploit? Identifying these vulnerabilities beforehand allows you to strengthen your case proactively, addressing these weaknesses before your opponent even brings them up. This proactive approach builds a stronger, more resilient case, reducing the likelihood of surprise attacks during the actual presentation.

More than simply identifying weaknesses, however, this process demands you develop strategies to counter those anticipated criticisms. For each potential attack, brainstorm several responses. This thorough preparation provides you with flexible options, allowing you to tailor your response based on the context of the actual rebuttal. For instance, a preemptive explanation might defuse a damaging point, turning a potential weakness into a minor detail.

Alternatively, a direct refutation, supported by strong evidence, might dismantle the opposing argument altogether. Flexibility is crucial.

Addressing potential rebuttals doesn't solely involve defensive strategies; it also informs your presentation's structure. By strategically placing information, you can preemptively address likely counterarguments before they're even raised. Consider weaving anticipatory elements into your main points; this allows you to proactively address and disarm potential criticisms before the opposition has a chance to highlight them. This seamless integration makes your presentation stronger and more persuasive.

Finally, remember the power of a strategic concession. Acknowledging a minor point in the opposition's favor can actually strengthen your overall position. It demonstrates fairness and intellectual honesty. This approach, often underutilized, can diffuse much of the opposition's energy by removing the need for them to spend time proving that self-evident point, allowing you to focus on the core aspects of your case. A carefully chosen concession can be a powerful weapon in your arsenal, shifting the focus away from minor disagreements and towards the significant aspects of your argument. It's a display of confidence and control that can significantly affect the outcome.

By consistently practicing these techniques, you transform the act of anticipating rebuttals from a daunting task into a strategic advantage. It's a crucial skill separating a proficient advocate from a truly exceptional one. This proactive approach allows for a more confident, persuasive, and ultimately, more successful presentation. The ability to anticipate your opponent's tactics is not merely a useful skill; it's the cornerstone of effective legal advocacy.

5.2 Strategic Concession

Strategic concession isn't about admitting defeat; it's a powerful tactical maneuver. It involves acknowledging the validity of certain aspects of the opposing argument, thereby demonstrating fairness, intelligence, and a nuanced understanding of the case. This approach, far from weakening your position, can actually strengthen it. By conceding minor points, you build credibility and trust with the judge or jury, making them more receptive to your central arguments. They'll perceive you not as someone trying to bury the truth, but as someone presenting a well-reasoned and complete picture of the situation. Think of it as a strategic retreat to gain a better vantage point for the final assault.

However, the choice of what to concede is crucial. Don't concede core arguments or essential facts; only acknowledge minor points that don't undermine your overall case. Perhaps the opposing counsel has presented evidence supporting a tangential aspect of the case, an aspect that while not directly relevant to your central claims, doesn't contradict them. Conceding this could significantly deflate their perceived impact, as it shows you're not afraid to admit what's demonstrably true, even if it doesn't serve your primary objectives. This builds your integrity.

Conceding also allows you to control the narrative. You can frame the concession in a way that redirects the attention back to your stronger points. For instance, you might concede a minor detail, then immediately pivot to emphasize how this detail, while seemingly detrimental, actually supports your overall theory. This skillful maneuver reframes a potentially negative element into something supportive or at least neutral. Mastering this involves careful planning and a deep understanding of your case, anticipating the possible counterarguments and preparing appropriate responses to strategically concede and immediately shift focus.

Remember, the goal isn't just to concede, it's to concede effectively. Don't make your concession a lengthy, rambling affair; keep it concise and to the point. A brief acknowledgement, smoothly integrated into your larger argument, is far more effective than a lengthy, drawn-out admission that risks losing the audience's attention or, worse, appearing overly apologetic or uncertain. Aim for succinctness; a well-placed, brief concession can be far more powerful than a lengthy explanation.

Furthermore, consider the emotional impact of your concession. A genuine concession, made with sincerity and without defensiveness, can be disarming. It shows humility and confidence—a powerful combination. Conversely, a reluctant or grudging concession can backfire, casting doubt on your credibility. Your demeanor is as important as the words themselves; your body language should reflect honesty and confidence, even as you concede a point to your opponent.

In practice, consider a personal injury case where the plaintiff claims significant emotional distress. Rather than entirely denying the claim, you might concede that the accident was undoubtedly upsetting. This concession, while acknowledging some distress, opens the door to highlight the lack of evidence for the plaintiff's claim of "significant" distress. You can then focus your arguments on the lack of objective evidence for the severity of the claimed emotional trauma. This approach displays reason and understanding while strategically positioning your arguments for the stronger points.

Another example might involve a contract dispute. Suppose the opposing counsel presents evidence suggesting a minor breach of contract on your client's part. Rather than outright denying it, you could concede the minor breach, but then emphasize that the breach was inconsequential and did not materially affect the overall agreement. You then redirect the discussion to emphasize the other party's more substantial breach of contract and how this breach constitutes a far more significant issue.

In summary, strategic concession is a sophisticated tool that, when used correctly, can significantly enhance your persuasive power. It allows you to control the narrative, build credibility, and highlight the strength of your central arguments, all while displaying fairness and reason. It's not about weakness, but about strategic strength – the art of gracefully acknowledging the valid points while reinforcing your stronger ones, leading to a more persuasive overall argument. Mastering this skill requires a deep understanding of your case and the ability to anticipate and preemptively manage counterarguments. By combining logical reasoning with an understanding of human psychology, you can transform a potential weakness into a strategic advantage, setting the stage for a winning argument.

5.3 Refuting Counterarguments

Directly confronting opposing arguments is crucial; avoiding them weakens your case. A well-constructed rebuttal doesn't simply dismiss the opposition; it dismantles it strategically, demonstrating a thorough understanding of the counterarguments while simultaneously reinforcing your own position. This requires careful preparation and a nuanced approach.

Begin by acknowledging the opposing argument's existence. Ignoring a strong counterpoint suggests weakness, not strength. Instead, briefly summarize the opposing viewpoint, demonstrating that you've considered it thoughtfully. This tactic, however, requires precision; avoid misrepresenting the opposing argument; accurately reflect their points to build credibility.

Then, systematically dissect the opposing argument. Look for flaws in its logic, inconsistencies in its evidence, or gaps in its reasoning. Perhaps the opposition relies on outdated case law, omits relevant facts, or misinterprets statutes. Highlight these weaknesses, using clear, concise language and providing concrete examples to support your critique. If a specific statistic or piece of evidence is presented, thoroughly explore it, potentially offering alternative interpretations or challenging the methodology.

Consider using analogies or hypothetical scenarios to illustrate the flaws in the opposing argument. A well-crafted analogy can simplify complex concepts, making your points more accessible and memorable. For instance, if the opposing argument relies on an overly broad interpretation of a legal principle, a simple analogy might reveal the absurdity of such a reading. The use of hypothetical scenarios helps apply legal principles to specific factual circumstances, emphasizing their practical limitations or applications.

Don't shy away from addressing the emotional appeal of the opposing argument, if it exists. While focusing on logic and evidence is paramount, acknowledging and countering the emotional aspects can significantly strengthen your rebuttal. The goal isn't to match the opponent's emotional intensity but to provide a reasoned, balanced response that addresses the emotional underpinnings of their argument while maintaining your composure and objectivity. However, it's key to maintain a professional demeanor; avoid resorting to personal attacks or inflammatory rhetoric.

Next, explicitly connect the weaknesses you've identified in the opposing argument to the strengths of your own. This isn't simply about contrasting the two; it's about showing how your position directly addresses the shortcomings of the opposing viewpoint. For example, if the opposing argument lacks relevant evidence, highlight the abundance of compelling evidence supporting your case. If their logic is flawed, emphasize the robustness and internal consistency of your own reasoning.

Finally, reiterate your own argument in light of the refuted counterarguments. This reinforces your main points and leaves a lasting impression. This isn't a simple repetition but a refined summary, integrating the insights gained from dismantling the opposing position. It shows a cohesive, well-considered approach to the entire case.

Remember, the goal is not to win at all costs, but to persuade through reasoned argumentation. A respectful, evidence-based approach not only strengthens your case but also enhances your credibility and professionalism. By following these steps, you can confidently address opposing viewpoints and strengthen the persuasiveness of your own. The ability to effectively refute counterarguments isn't just a legal skill; it's a crucial component of building a winning case. Mastering this skill significantly increases your chance of success in any legal proceeding. And remember, the strongest arguments anticipate potential objections and address them proactively, showing a thorough understanding of the entirety of the legal landscape surrounding the case. Therefore, a thorough understanding and preparation for refuting counterarguments is vital in building a strong and successful legal case.

6 Chapter 6: Visual Aids and Delivery

Visual aids aren't mere decorations; they're powerful tools to solidify your case. A well-crafted chart can illuminate complex financial transactions, transforming confusing numbers into easily digestible information. Similarly, a concise timeline can clarify the sequence of events, establishing causality and strengthening your narrative. Avoid clutter; simplicity reigns supreme. Each visual should serve a specific purpose, directly supporting a key argument. Think concisely and carefully, and always test your visuals beforehand. Ensure fonts are legible, colours are complementary, and the overall design is clean and professional, because even the best argument can be undermined by poor presentation.

Your voice is your instrument. A monotone delivery lulls the audience into apathy, while a vibrant, modulated voice holds attention and emphasizes key points. Practice varying your pace, tone, and volume; pauses for emphasis can be more powerful than words themselves. Enunciate clearly; mumbling undermines credibility. Record yourself practicing and identify areas for improvement. It's crucial to be comfortable in your vocal delivery. Confidence is key, and this is cultivated only through diligent practice.

Body language speaks volumes, often louder than words. Maintain confident eye contact, connecting with your audience individually, fostering a sense of engagement and rapport. Avoid fidgeting; stand tall with open posture, projecting confidence and authority. Gestures should be natural, reinforcing your message, not distracting from it. Mirroring your audience's posture subtly can create subconscious connection, facilitating trust and acceptance of your arguments. Pay close attention to the non-verbal cues you transmit. Remember, this is as important as what you say.

Handling Q&A is a critical skill, demanding composure and quick thinking. Listen carefully to each question, clarifying ambiguities before responding. If unsure of the answer, admit it honestly; it's better than fabricating a response. Use the opportunity to reiterate key points within your responses; weave answers naturally back into your arguments. Never get defensive. Maintain professionalism even when facing aggressive questioning. Consider the courtroom setting and anticipate difficult questions– preparation and practice are crucial for effective responses.

Nervousness is a common experience, affecting even seasoned advocates. Deep breathing exercises can calm your nerves before and during the presentation. Visualization, picturing a successful presentation, can build confidence. Preparation is your most potent antidote. Thoroughly rehearsing your arguments will reduce anxiety by building familiarity and confidence. Remember that some nerves are normal; channel this energy to become passionate and enthusiastic about your argument, rather than letting it impede your performance. Learn your material so well that you are relaxed and not tense.

6.1 Effective Visuals

Visual aids aren't mere embellishments; they are powerful tools shaping audience perception and comprehension. A well-crafted infographic, for instance, can instantly clarify complex data that would take pages of dense text to explain. Consider the impact of a timeline visually charting the events of a case, illustrating the chronology with clarity and immediacy. This is far more effective than simply narrating the events linearly. Remember, the human brain processes visual information significantly faster than text. Leverage this inherent advantage.

Effective visuals should always be strategically aligned with your overarching argument. Don't include a chart simply because you have data; ensure it supports a specific point you're trying to make. Perhaps you're demonstrating a pattern of behavior, a financial trend, or a geographical distribution. Whatever the data, the visual should directly reinforce your argument, adding weight and impact. Aim for visuals that are both informative and visually appealing, avoiding clutter and unnecessary detail.

Simplicity is key. Overly complex graphics are counterproductive; they confuse, rather than clarify. Think clean lines, clear fonts, and a restrained color palette. Use contrasting colors to emphasize key information but avoid a chaotic clash of hues. Your aim is to highlight important data, not to overwhelm your audience with visual stimuli. Remember, the visual is a supporting actor, not the star of the show. The focus must always remain on your argument.

Photographs can be exceptionally persuasive, especially when dealing with physical evidence or illustrating the impact of events. A well-chosen photograph of a damaged property, for example, can speak volumes, conveying the scale of the damage and its emotional impact far more powerfully than any written description. However, ensure the photograph is of high quality and relevant to the case. Avoid blurry or poorly lit images that diminish their impact. Always ensure that you have the legal right to use any photograph or image you incorporate into your presentation.

Avoid generic stock images; they lack authenticity and often detract from the overall presentation. Use visuals that are specific to your case and tailored to the audience's understanding. If you are presenting to a technical audience, you may use more detailed charts and graphs than if you were presenting to a jury. Adapt your visuals to the specific context and knowledge level of your audience. Remember, the goal isn't to impress with technical prowess but to effectively communicate your message.

Remember the principle of "show, don't tell." Instead of stating a statistic, present it visually using a bar chart or pie chart. Instead of describing the location of an event, use a map to pinpoint it geographically. This principle applies to every aspect of your visual aids. By showing, rather than telling, you create a more memorable and persuasive presentation. Think carefully about the format of each visual; each should be meticulously designed to communicate precisely what you need to say.

The selection of visual aids should be guided by practicality. Consider the context of your presentation. A courtroom setting necessitates different visual aids than a negotiation room. For instance, in a courtroom you might opt for large, clear displays that are easily visible to all. In contrast, a smaller, more intimate setting might allow for handouts or interactive presentations. Your preparation should always take into account the practical aspects of the location and the audience's accessibility needs.

Above all, ensure your visuals are integrated seamlessly into your presentation. They should complement, not detract from, your spoken argument. Avoid simply reading from your slides; instead, use the visuals as prompts to elaborate on key points and engage your audience. Practice your presentation thoroughly, ensuring that your verbal delivery synchronizes smoothly with your visual aids. This will result in a coherent, compelling presentation that will leave a lasting impression on your audience. Ultimately, the success of your presentation rests not only on the strength of your argument but also on the effectiveness of your visual communication.

6.2 Vocal Delivery

Your voice is your instrument. It's the medium through which your carefully constructed arguments take flight, resonating with the judge, jury, or client. A strong vocal delivery isn't merely about speaking clearly; it's about commanding attention, conveying emotion, and fostering trust. Mastering it is crucial to presenting a winning case.

Think of your voice as a brush, painting a picture with words. Vary your tone, your pace, and your inflection to highlight crucial points and maintain audience engagement. A monotonous drone will quickly lose your listener, no matter how brilliant your legal reasoning. Inflection, the rise and fall of your pitch, adds colour and nuance to your words, emphasizing key evidence and making your argument more memorable.

Articulation is paramount. Ensure every word is crisp and clear, avoiding mumbled phrases or slurred speech. Practice enunciating, paying attention to consonants and vowels. Record yourself delivering a portion of your argument–it's a surprisingly effective tool for self-assessment. Identify areas needing improvement, and deliberately work on those aspects in subsequent practice sessions. Aim for a vocal delivery that is both natural and polished, reflecting your confidence in the strength of your case.

Pause strategically. Silence, appropriately used, can be as powerful as words. A well-timed pause allows your audience to absorb important information, adding weight to your arguments. It also helps you maintain composure and control during intense questioning or when delivering sensitive information. Don't be afraid of the silence; use it to your advantage. Employ pauses to create dramatic effect or emphasize a critical point, creating anticipation and reinforcing the impact of your statements. The careful use of pauses punctuates your argument, akin to the punctuation in a well-crafted written brief.

Volume control is just as important. A consistent, moderate volume ensures your message is heard clearly, but it's vital to modulate your voice to suit the context. A lower, more intimate tone can create a connection with your audience during emotionally charged moments, while a slightly elevated volume can emphasize key points or counter a challenging assertion. Avoid shouting – it often sounds aggressive and undermines your credibility. Instead, find ways to use subtle variations in volume to control the narrative flow and engage different aspects of your audience's attention.

Pace yourself. Speaking too quickly can make it difficult for your audience to follow your argument, whilst speaking too slowly can be equally ineffective. Find a natural rhythm that suits both your style and the material you are presenting. Vary the pace to keep your audience engaged. Accelerate slightly when emphasizing a particularly compelling piece of evidence or a crucial point in your argument. Slow down for key definitions or complex details requiring careful consideration. The pace of your speech should reflect the emotional and intellectual rhythm of your argument, creating a natural ebb and flow that will keep your audience engaged. It's a subtle yet powerful element of effective delivery.

Practice, practice, practice. There is no substitute for rehearsal. The more familiar you are with your material, the more confident and natural your delivery will be. Practice in front of a mirror, record yourself, and solicit feedback from trusted colleagues or mentors. This iterative process of refinement will significantly enhance your ability to deliver your arguments with clarity, conviction, and passion. Each practice session allows you to hone your delivery, refine your pacing, and adjust your tone to ensure optimal impact and engagement with your intended audience. Through repetition, the presentation becomes less an act of performance and more an act of informed communication.

6.3 Body Language

Your posture speaks volumes before you even utter a word. Slouching conveys disinterest and a lack of confidence, potentially undermining your credibility from the outset. Stand tall, shoulders back, but maintain a natural, relaxed stance. Avoid rigidity; stiffness can appear artificial and untrustworthy. Imagine yourself as a confident, capable advocate–project that image physically. This visual display of assurance will subtly influence the perception of your argument.

Maintaining eye contact is paramount, but it's a delicate balance. Stare intensely at one person for too long and you risk intimidation. Shift your gaze naturally among the judge, jury, and opposing counsel–establishing connections without fixating. Brief glances away to gather your thoughts are acceptable, even beneficial, demonstrating thoughtfulness rather than evasion. Remember, your eyes are a window to your soul; let them reflect honesty and engagement.

Gestures should enhance, not distract. Avoid excessive hand movements; wild flapping can be unsettling and appear insincere. Use controlled, deliberate movements to emphasize key points, mirroring the rhythm of your speech. Open palms signify honesty and openness, while clenched fists might be perceived as aggression. Think of your body as an instrument, conducting the orchestra of your argument with precision and grace. Consider the impact of your movements.

Facial expressions are equally critical; they must align with your words and tone. A genuine smile can disarm and build rapport, while a furrowed brow might convey doubt or uncertainty, even if your argument is ironclad. Practice your facial expressions; mirrors can be helpful in refining this aspect of non-verbal communication. This requires active attention. Remember this is a practice that benefits not only your legal career but your social life in general.

The space you occupy also contributes to your overall presence. Don't hover nervously near the edge of the room. Own your space, move with purpose, and occupy the courtroom with confidence. Your physical presence should command attention without being overly aggressive. This confidence is often overlooked by inexperienced advocates, who can sometimes be so nervous that their body language speaks volumes, and mostly, unfortunately, counterproductive to their argument. A deliberate walk from your podium to display a key exhibit, for instance, can add weight to its importance.

Mirroring (subtly) the body language of the judge or jury can foster a sense of connection and rapport. If they lean forward attentively, subtly mirroring their posture can unconsciously create a bond, making them more receptive to your argument. However, mirroring should be done subtly and not overtly; excessive imitation would seem disingenuous and likely counterproductive. This is about building understanding, not about creating a comedy sketch. Instead, let your body language complement your argument, working in synergy to achieve your goals. Remember, body language is an intricate dance; practice and refinement are key to mastering its subtle art. It's a craft to be honed over time.

Finally, remember that self-awareness is the cornerstone of effective body language. Record yourself presenting; analyze your posture, gestures, and facial expressions. Seek feedback from trusted colleagues or mentors; their insights can identify areas for improvement that you may have missed. Consistent self-reflection and refinement are crucial for honing your non-verbal communication skills, and your courtroom presence. Becoming adept at this crucial skill will significantly enhance your ability to win your case.

6.4 Q&A Strategies

Mastering the Q&A session is crucial; it's your opportunity to solidify your argument, address concerns, and demonstrate your command of the subject matter. Remember, the questions aren't an attack; they're an invitation to further clarify your position and showcase your expertise. Prepare for common questions related to your case; anticipate potential weaknesses and craft concise, persuasive responses. Doing so will increase your credibility and build confidence.

Begin by listening attentively. Understanding the question fully is paramount before formulating your response. Don't interrupt; let the questioner finish completely. Pause before answering, even for a moment, to gather your thoughts and ensure a well-structured reply. This demonstrates composure and allows you to tailor your response precisely to the question asked.

If the question is unclear or ambiguous, don't hesitate to politely request clarification. A simple "Could you rephrase that question?" or "I want to ensure I understand your question correctly..." can be incredibly effective. This avoids misunderstandings and allows you to provide a more accurate and relevant response. It also shows the judge or jury your attentiveness to detail and your commitment to accuracy.

Structure your answers logically and concisely. Avoid rambling; get to the point quickly. Use clear, simple language that everyone can understand, even those without legal expertise. Prioritize precision and avoid legal jargon unless absolutely necessary, and then explain its meaning clearly. A well-structured response, delivered clearly and confidently, resonates far more effectively than a long, convoluted explanation.

Use the opportunity to reinforce key arguments from your case. If a question presents an opening, skillfully weave your response to highlight previously presented evidence or reiterate crucial points. This reinforces your narrative and keeps your primary message front and center. Every response should be a strategic opportunity to bolster your overall case.

Handle challenging or hostile questions with grace and professionalism. Never show anger or frustration, even when faced with aggressive questioning. Maintain your composure and respond directly to the question, addressing the concerns raised without resorting to defensiveness. Instead, acknowledge their concerns and respectfully offer a counterpoint or clarification.

For questions you don't know the answer to, admit it honestly. It's far better to acknowledge a lack of knowledge than to attempt a false answer. You can say, "That's a good question. I don't have the answer readily available, but I will be happy to provide it at a later time." Then follow up diligently to provide the information. This shows your integrity and willingness to seek answers.

Finally, practice your Q&A skills extensively. Conduct mock Q&A sessions with colleagues or mentors. This will help you anticipate tough questions and refine your responses. This preparation will translate to greater confidence and effectiveness during the actual Q&A session, allowing you to handle any question confidently and professionally. Effective Q&A preparation is an investment in the success of your case.

6.5 Managing Nervousness

Nervousness is a common experience for even the most seasoned lawyers. It's a physiological response, a surge of adrenaline preparing you for a demanding situation. Understanding this helps demystify the feeling, making it less daunting. Instead of fighting it, acknowledge its presence; it's your body's way of saying, "This is important!" Channel that energy into focused preparation and confident delivery.

Proper preparation is the most effective antidote to performance anxiety. Thorough research, meticulous organization of your arguments, and a well-rehearsed presentation significantly reduce the likelihood of unexpected surprises. Know your material inside and out; anticipate potential questions and formulate clear, concise answers. This proactive approach builds confidence, minimizing the impact of nerves during the actual presentation. Rehearse not just the content but also the delivery; practice in front of a mirror, record yourself, or even present to trusted colleagues for feedback. Every rehearsal reinforces your familiarity and smooths out potential stumbling blocks. This reduces your fear of the unknown during the presentation. The more prepared you are, the more you'll feel in control. This control will translate into a calm, confident demeanor.

Visualize success. Before your presentation, spend a few minutes actively imagining yourself delivering a confident and compelling argument. Envision a positive outcome, focusing on the positive aspects of the experience rather than dwelling on the potential pitfalls. This mental rehearsal is a powerful tool, helping you replace anxious thoughts with confident visualizations. This positive reinforcement primes your mind for success, replacing fear with a sense of preparedness and capability. The more vividly you visualize success, the more likely it is to become a self-fulfilling prophecy. Your mind and body will naturally react to your visualization, mirroring your imagined confidence.

Physical preparation is just as important as mental preparation. Get a good night's sleep before your presentation. Eat a healthy meal, avoiding excessive caffeine or sugar. Engage in some light exercise to release tension and improve blood flow. These simple yet effective practices help optimize your physical and mental state, enhancing your ability to focus and perform at your best. A healthy lifestyle is the foundation for effective performance. Neglecting physical wellbeing can negatively impact your presentation, even beyond simple tiredness. Aim for a healthy body and a healthy mind to achieve a successful performance.

Deep breathing exercises are invaluable tools for managing nervousness. Practice controlled breathing techniques before and during your presentation. Inhale deeply, hold for a few seconds, and exhale slowly. This simple exercise helps regulate your heart rate and calm your nervous system. Deep breathing can be done discreetly, providing an immediate method to manage anxiety in the heat of the moment. It's a quick and effective way to regulate your nervous system and re-center your focus. This is particularly helpful during Q&A sessions where unexpected questions might arise.

Engage in positive self-talk. Instead of focusing on your fears, remind yourself of your strengths and accomplishments. Affirm your capabilities and competence. Positive self-talk helps shift your perspective from anxiety to confidence. Replacing negative thoughts with positive affirmations will boost your mood and improve your presentation. These positive affirmations can be tailored to your specific situation, and even a few short sentences can have a remarkable impact on your confidence. It is a simple yet powerful technique.

Remember that nervousness is normal and even expected in high-stakes situations. It's a sign that you care about your work and that you're invested in the outcome. It's not a sign of weakness but of your dedication to this important task. Embracing this understanding reduces the pressure you place on yourself, transforming the experience from something to be feared to something to be acknowledged and managed. This shift in perspective will lessen your anxiety significantly. Acknowledge the feeling, manage it strategically, and focus on your successful delivery.

7 Chapter 7: Winning Strategies & Tactics

Maintaining ethical conduct is paramount in legal practice. Upholding the integrity of the profession requires adherence to strict codes of conduct, which vary by jurisdiction but universally emphasize honesty, fairness, and respect for the court. Understanding these rules is not just a matter of avoiding sanctions; it's fundamental to building trust with the court and opposing counsel, fostering a climate of fairness that benefits all parties involved. A lawyer's reputation, built on consistent ethical behavior, is their most valuable asset. Negligence in this area can not only lead to disciplinary actions but also irrevocably damage your credibility.

Effective trial techniques extend beyond simply presenting evidence. They encompass strategic decision-making at every stage, from jury selection to closing arguments. Consider jury selection, a crucial step often overlooked. Understanding the demographics and potential biases of potential jurors allows for strategic challenges, helping to assemble a jury more sympathetic to your client's case. Meticulous preparation and insightful questioning are vital for maximizing the impact of your witnesses' testimony. Anticipating the opposing counsel's line of questioning and preparing your witnesses accordingly is crucial in mitigating potential damage.

Opening statements should not merely summarize the facts; they must paint a compelling narrative, engaging the jury from the outset and setting the stage for the rest of the trial. This initial impression is critical; it sets the tone and influences how the jury will perceive subsequent evidence. Similarly, closing arguments should not simply reiterate the evidence but weave together the narrative, highlighting the key takeaways and emphasizing the crucial points that support your client's case. A strong closing argument should leave a lasting impression, effectively summarizing the case and persuading the jury of your client's position.

Effective cross-examination is more than just asking questions; it's a delicate dance of strategic probing and controlled aggression. The goal is not just to expose weaknesses in the opposing witness's testimony, but also to discredit their credibility. This requires careful planning, anticipating potential responses, and framing questions in a manner that highlights contradictions or inconsistencies. The art of cross-examination lies in its subtlety, using leading questions to guide the witness toward the desired conclusion while avoiding giving them the opportunity to elaborate or evade the point. Effective cross-examination can be the difference between success and failure.

Understanding the nuances of evidentiary rules is vital for a successful outcome. Knowing what evidence is admissible, and how to present it effectively, can make or break your case. Objections, when used strategically, can control the flow of the trial and prevent damaging information from being presented to the jury. However, excessive or frivolous objections can undermine your credibility, so timing and precision are key. Mastering these aspects of trial procedure requires both theoretical knowledge and practical experience; the ability to apply legal principles in real-time distinguishes successful advocates.

Beyond courtroom tactics, building a strong case hinges on diligent preparation. Thorough investigation and comprehensive research are the foundations upon which successful legal arguments are built. This meticulous approach is crucial; it's the bedrock of a persuasive case. This includes not only gathering evidence but also anticipating potential challenges and crafting responses. A well-prepared case allows for greater flexibility and responsiveness during the trial, empowering you to adapt to unexpected circumstances. The more prepared you are, the less likely you are to be caught off-guard. This comprehensive preparation is the key to building a strong and ultimately successful case. A successful outcome depends not only on effective courtroom strategies but also on the foundational work undertaken before the trial even begins.

Remember, winning strategies are not solely about legal prowess; they're deeply intertwined with understanding human psychology. Appealing to the jury's emotions, while remaining within ethical boundaries, can profoundly influence their perception of the case. Empathy and understanding of their perspective are key; you are not simply presenting legal arguments, but telling a story that resonates with their values and experiences. Therefore, tailoring your arguments to connect with their sensibilities is a powerful tool for achieving a favorable outcome. Successfully navigating the complexities of legal argumentation requires not only a strong grasp of the law but also a sophisticated understanding of human nature.

Finally, throughout the trial, maintain professionalism and composure. Even under pressure, conduct yourself with dignity and respect. The way you present yourself can significantly influence the jury's perception of your client's case. This professional demeanor contributes to a perception of competence and trustworthiness, reinforcing the credibility of your arguments. Maintaining composure, even in the face of unexpected challenges, demonstrates a strong command of the situation and instills confidence in your ability to effectively represent your client's interests. The final verdict is often influenced as much by your demeanor as your legal arguments.

7.1 Legal Ethics

Maintaining ethical conduct is paramount in legal practice; it's the bedrock upon which trust and the integrity of the justice system are built. Your reputation, built on consistent ethical behavior, is as valuable, if not more so, than any single case win. Remember, shortcuts often lead to long-term damage, both professionally and personally. Ethical lapses can lead to disbarment, hefty fines, and the irreparable erosion of public trust, consequences far outweighing any perceived short-term gain.

The rules of professional conduct, though sometimes complex, provide a clear framework for navigating ethical dilemmas. Familiarize yourself with your jurisdiction's specific rules; they're not merely suggestions, but binding obligations. Understanding these rules is not enough; you must actively internalize them, making ethical considerations an integral part of every decision you make. Don't just passively read the rules; engage with them, study them, and discuss them with colleagues – creating a professional network where ethical discussions are commonplace.

Confidentiality is a cornerstone of legal ethics. Client information, even seemingly insignificant details, is protected by attorney-client privilege. This privilege extends beyond active representation; past clients' confidences remain protected. Breaching this confidentiality can have serious repercussions, harming not just your client but also the trust placed in the legal profession as a whole. Remember, accidental disclosures, too, can have damaging consequences. Implement robust security measures to protect client data, and always seek advice when faced with a situation you aren't sure how to handle ethically.

Conflicts of interest present another significant ethical challenge. Representing clients with opposing interests, even tangentially, creates a clear conflict. You must diligently assess potential conflicts before accepting a new client, even if it means forgoing potentially lucrative cases. Transparency is crucial; disclose any potential conflicts promptly and fully to all affected parties, allowing them to make informed decisions. Ignoring or downplaying conflicts not only jeopardizes your ethical standing but also undermines your ability to provide effective representation. Seeking external advice, when necessary, to ensure your actions remain ethically sound is prudent practice.

Diligence and competence are not just abstract ideals; they are ethical obligations. You are responsible for thoroughly researching your cases, keeping up-to-date with legal developments, and providing competent representation within your area of expertise. Failing to do so not only risks jeopardizing your client's case but also breaches your ethical duty. Continuing legal education is not an option but a necessity. Regularly engaging in professional development shows your commitment to upholding ethical standards and ensures you possess the necessary skills to effectively serve your clients.

Objectivity is crucial. While zealous advocacy is expected, it mustn't morph into dishonesty or misrepresentation. Present your client's case honestly and accurately, relying on solid evidence and sound legal arguments. Avoid making unsubstantiated claims or exaggerating facts. Respect opposing counsel and the court; civility and professionalism are not merely polite gestures but demonstrate ethical commitment. Remember that your role is to advocate for justice, not to win at all costs. Striving for fairness and integrity in every interaction is as important as winning the case itself.

Finally, remember that ethical dilemmas are rarely clear-cut. When faced with a difficult situation, consult with experienced colleagues, seek ethical opinions, or consider referring the matter to an ethics committee. Transparency and seeking guidance are not signs of weakness, but rather hallmarks of responsible professional conduct. Continuously evaluating your actions and ensuring compliance with ethical guidelines is a journey, not a destination. Maintaining the highest ethical standards isn't just a matter of following rules; it's about upholding the dignity and integrity of the legal profession, ensuring fairness and justice for all. Your commitment to ethical practice reflects not only on you but on the entire legal system.

7.2 Trial Techniques

Effective cross-examination hinges on preparation. Thoroughly review all discovery materials, focusing not just on what the witness says, but also on what they don't say. Identify inconsistencies, contradictions, and gaps in their testimony, preparing pointed questions to expose these weaknesses. This isn't about aggression; it's about revealing the truth through careful questioning. Remember, a seemingly insignificant detail could unravel the opposition's entire case. Use your preparation meticulously; it will be your most potent weapon.

Effective opening statements are more than just a summary of facts. They paint a picture, setting the stage for the entire trial. Think of it as a carefully crafted narrative, introducing your client and their story with empathy and precision. Avoid legal jargon; speak in clear, concise language that resonates with the jury. A compelling opening statement isn't about overwhelming the jury with details; it's about capturing their attention and setting the tone for what's to come, making them eager to hear more.

Direct examination needs to be concise and clear. Lead your witnesses with well-structured questions, allowing them to present their testimony in a logical, compelling manner. Avoid open-ended questions that could allow the witness to wander off-topic or reveal damaging information. Practice beforehand to ensure the flow of questions is natural and effective, mirroring the natural progression of the events you are presenting, thus enhancing coherence and clarity. Trust your preparation; you've built a solid foundation.

Jury selection is crucial. Understand that each prospective juror is an individual with unique experiences and perspectives. Pay close attention to their answers during voir dire, looking beyond simple yes or no responses to their nuances. You need to look at their body language, the tone of their voice and how well their answers match the questions you ask. Identifying potential biases and sympathetic jurors requires keen observation and insightful questioning, skills only honed through experience. Your intuition matters, but let facts lead your choices.

Effective closing arguments synthesize the evidence presented throughout the trial, weaving together a coherent and persuasive narrative. It is where all the efforts meet. This isn't a time to introduce new evidence. Instead, it's an opportunity to remind the jury of the key points, tying them back to your opening statement and emphasizing the strength of your case. Speak with conviction and passion, leaving the jury with a clear understanding of why your client should prevail, invoking a sense of justice that aligns with your arguments.

Managing objections requires skill and strategy. Don't interrupt unnecessarily, and remember, an objection overruled is likely to annoy the judge and backfire on you. Choose your objections judiciously, only raising them when truly necessary. The goal is not to obstruct the opposing counsel, but to maintain the integrity of the trial and ensure a fair hearing. Remember your goal: justice served, not just victory. This demands composure and patience.

Knowing when to rest is important. Don't over-extend your case by presenting unnecessary evidence or prolonging arguments. A concise, well-structured presentation is more effective than one that is convoluted and meandering. Know when to stop presenting evidence; too much information can muddy the waters and confuse the jury, ultimately harming your case. Trust the preparation you've already put in, and make sure to only show what is necessary.

Preparation is paramount for success in any trial. This isn't just about legal research and witness preparation; it also encompasses understanding the judge, jury and the courtroom procedures. Anticipate potential challenges and formulate strategic responses. The better you understand the entire landscape of the trial, the better you will be able to adapt to changing circumstances and effectively present your case. Remember, this isn't just about memorizing rules and procedures; it's about understanding the underlying principles of justice.

www.ingramcontent.com/pod-product-compliance
Lightning Source LLC
LaVergne TN
LVHW022021200926
848481LV00007B/2474
9798348581763